DATE DUE			

6853

574.5
SCH

Schoonmaker, Peter
K.

The living forest.

MESA VERDE MIDDLE SCHOOL
POWAY UNIFIED SCHOOL DISTRICT

The Living
FOREST

Peter K. Schoonmaker

The Living World Series

ENSLOW PUBLISHERS, INC.

Bloy St. & Ramsey Ave.
Box 777
Hillside, N.J. 07205
U.S.A.

P.O. Box 38
Aldershot
Hants GU12 6BP
U.K.

Library of Congress Cataloging-in-Publication Data

Schoonmaker, Peter K.
    The Living Forest / by Peter K. Schoonmaker.
        p. cm.— (The Living world series)
    Bibliography: p.
    Includes index.
    Summary: Examines the characteristics of the vegetation found in
    temperate and boreal (far northern) forests discussing their
    ecological significance and importance to people.
    ISBN 0-89490-270-9
    1. Forest ecology—Juvenile literature. 2. Forests and forestry—Juvenile
    literature. 3. Forest ecology—North America—Juvenile
    literature. 4. Forests and forestry—North America—Juvenile
    literature. [1. Forests and forestry. 2. Forest ecology.
    3. Ecology.] I. Title. II. Series.
    QK938.F6S36 1990
    574.5'2642—dc20   89-33603
                                                        CIP
                                                         AC

Printed in the United States of America

10 9 8 7 6 5 4 3 2

Illustration Credits:
Bill Byrne, pp. 20, 47; Eric Forsman, p. 38; D.R. Foster, pp. 19, 22; Forest History
Society, p. 55; Harvard Forest Archives, p. 6; Ellen Moriarty, pp. 4, 10, 11, 28, 49;
National Agricultural Library, Forest Service Photo Collection, pp. 14, 26, 30, 34, 40,
56; Peter K. Schoonmaker, pp. 7, 18, 44, 53 59; U.S. Forest Service, p. 13; Ted
Thomas, p. 37.

Cover Photo: U.S. Forest Service.

Contents

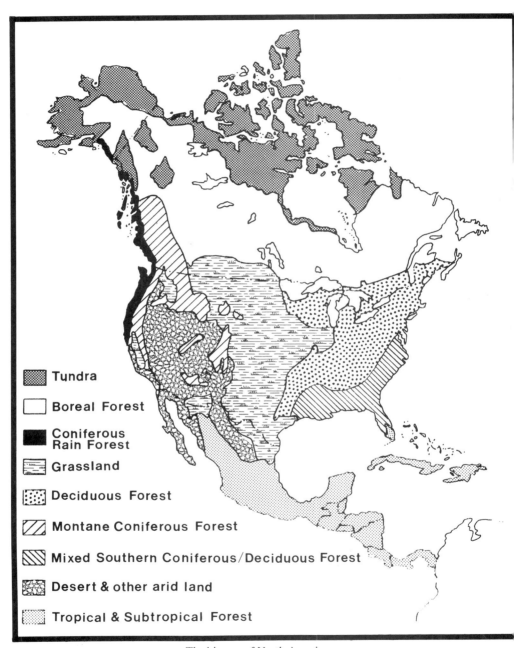

Tundra

Boreal Forest

Coniferous Rain Forest

Grassland

Deciduous Forest

Montane Coniferous Forest

Mixed Southern Coniferous/Deciduous Forest

Desert & other arid land

Tropical & Subtropical Forest

The biomes of North America.

Introduction

On a cool autumn day a young man climbs to the highest point on Manhattan Island, scrambling over massive trunks of oak, chestnut, hickory, and pine blown down in a recent wind storm. He swings himself up onto a huge log 6 feet in diameter. From here he can see above the surrounding shrubs that have taken over the open space once occupied by trees. Recently arrived in the New World from his native Amsterdam, he gazes westward across the Hudson River to the wooded cliffs and rolling hills on the other side.

In the distance several thin curtains of smoke rise up into the sky; Indians are burning the forest to make better habitat for the animals they hunt. Beyond the horizon lies an unknown land. It is 1650, more than a hundred years before the young man's descendants will fight in the Revolutionary War and found a new nation. He has no idea that the forest he sees stretches for a thousand miles to the Mississippi River and beyond. Or that most of it will be gone in three hundred years.

If he could walk across North America, he would notice that the deciduous forest in the East gives way to grasslands in the Midwest up to the Rocky Mountains, and that the various types of coniferous forest in the Rockies are followed by desert and shrubland between the Rockies and the Sierras. He would probably also notice that the towering coniferous forests along most of the west coast are unlike any forest he has ever seen.

Today we would also recognize these very different kinds of vegetation, or biomes. Forests still cover much of eastern North America. But they are very different from those found by the first settlers. Europeans converted thousands of square miles of forest into farmland, towns, and cities. Most of the remaining forests have been cut down and the wood used for more buildings, furniture, fuel, and

Large old trees like these white pines and hemlocks in New Hampshire were common when Europeans first arrived in North America.

6

paper products. The woods we see today are mostly second growth, composed of trees that have taken the place of the original forest. Many forests have even reclaimed old fields that were once farmed.

In western North America, more of the original presettlement forest still stands. Although these forests have been logged extensively during the twentieth century, enough remains for botanists to get a good idea of what the natural vegetation was like. You can walk for miles, surrounded by giant trunks of Douglas fir, hemlock, redwood,

The stone wall in this forest is evidence that this land was once farmed but then abandoned.

and other conifers whose towering canopies cast the same deep shade they did when Lewis and Clark first spied them two centuries ago. In general, humans have changed the forests of North America less than in many other places in the world. Still, one wonders what these forests were like when only Native Americans roamed the land.

In this book we will explore major forest biomes north of the tropics, using examples drawn from the forests of North America. A biome is a structurally distinct group of plants and animals on a continent. Tundra, temperate grassland, and tropical rain forest are examples of biomes. Although the term includes characteristic animals, biome usually refers to the type of vegetation. Plant geographers recognize six basic structural types of vegetation: forest, woodland, grassland, shrubland, semidesert scrub, and desert.

Forests cover about one-third of the world's land area, but they account for 90 percent of all plant material by weight (biomass) on earth. Almost half of the world's forests are found in the tropics, and about one-quarter grow in the far north, or boreal areas. Another 25 percent are temperate forests, found between the tropics and the far north.

Each year, the 1,650 billion tons of biomass contained in the world's forests grow another 74 billion tons of leaves, flowers, wood, and roots. Much of this biomass is either eaten by animals or dies and is consumed by decomposers (fungi, bacteria, insects). Humans use about 2 billion tons of wood each year, half for lumber and paper, and the other half for fuel. But we also cut down vast areas of forest every year, not to harvest the wood but to plant crops, build roads, and expand cities and towns. Some forests are even destroyed because of careless logging and farming practices, creating shrublands and deserts which will be difficult to restore.

The misuse of some of the world's forests is a tragedy. Plants are the basis of all life on earth: they harvest the sun's energy and pass it on to other organisms. Forest trees account for most of the plant matter on the planet, and it is hard to imagine life as we know it without forests. They control erosion, harvest energy, cycle nutrients, and influence local and global climate. They harbor thousands of useful plants and animals, and they provide food, fuel, and shelter for billions of people.

For these reasons we want to know where forests grow and why they grow there. First, we need to know how to recognize different kinds of forests.

Describing a Forest

Most of us know a forest when we see one. But there are many different types of forest—tropical, temperate, boreal, and so forth. How do we tell one from another? Forest ecologists distinguish forests by their composition and their structure.

The composition of a forest is what it is made of. When we talk about composition we want to know three things: (1) which growth forms (such as herbs, shrubs, trees) are present; (2) which species (for example, red maple, lodgepole pine, Douglas fir) are present; and (3) how much of each there is.

Structure means the way plants are distributed horizontally along the ground and vertically up into the canopy. Plants can be spaced regularly as in a grid, randomly, or in a clumped pattern. Usually plants are clumped, but this depends on the type of forest.

Vertical structure is one of the most distinctive characteristics of forests. Trees are called dominant if they reach the top of the canopy and get sun from all sides. The trees just below the very tallest ones are co-dominant. Trees are intermediate if they reach up a little into the canopy, and suppressed if they live even closer to the ground in the deep shade created by the larger trees above them. Many small trees actually thrive in the shady cool environment under the main canopy.

The lowest vertical layers of a forest are usually occupied by shrubs, young trees (saplings), and finally, closest to the ground, herbs, seedlings (trees that have just germinated from seed), and mosses.

A forest may contain any combination of these vertical layers. Some coniferous forests contain only dominant and co-dominant trees. Tropical rain forests often have several distinct stories, or layers.

Armed with the concepts of composition and structure, forest ecologists have described many types of forests. One of the first distinctions that ecologists make between different forests is evergreen coniferous versus broadleaved deciduous. Most forests north of the tropics fall into one of these categories. We will explain these terms

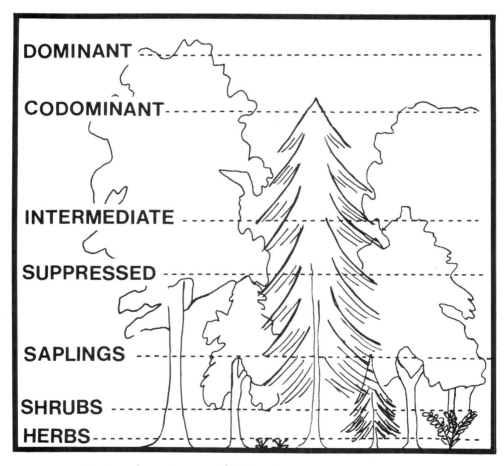

DOMINANT

CODOMINANT

INTERMEDIATE

SUPPRESSED

SAPLINGS

SHRUBS

HERBS

Forests may contain some or all of these layers of trees and other plants.

as we explore evergreen coniferous forests in Chapters 2 and 3, and deciduous forests in Chapters 4 and 5.

Distribution: Trees and Their Environment

Why do forests grow where they do? Why, for example, do we find similar deciduous forests growing in eastern North America and eastern Asia? And why do these forests give way to grasslands, shrublands and deserts to their west? The answer is complex, but we can boil it down to two parts.

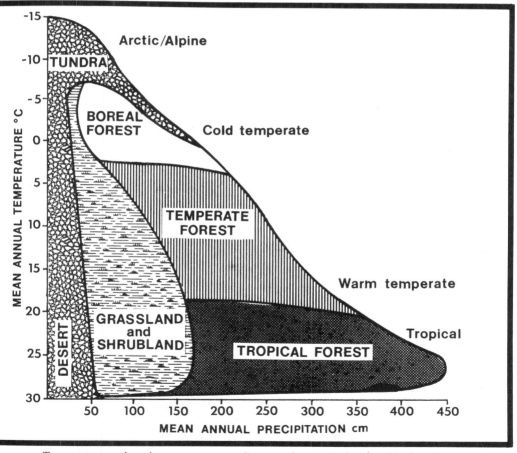

Temperature and moisture are among the most important factors affecting the distribution of vegetation.

11

First, each species of tree uses light, water, and nutrients different-ly. The way each species uses these resources explains why certain trees grow in one place, but not in another. One tree species may have many shallow roots and absorb water quickly. Another may flourish in the shade because it needs very little of the sun's energy to stay alive.

Second, many widely separated places in the world have very similar environments. And these similar environments support similar vegetation. But exactly what are the environmental factors that deter-mine the distribution of forests around the world? Temperature and moisture are probably the most important. But so are soil, disturbances such as fire and wind, and interaction with other organisms.

We all know that the earth's climate changes from warm to cold as we travel from the equator to the poles, and from sea level to high mountain peaks. In fact, if you were at the equator and climbed about 330 feet (100 meters) up from sea level, the temperature change would be about equal to that if you traveled north about 62 miles (100 kilometers).

Rainfall patterns around the world are controlled by global air and ocean circulation. The result is that most continents have fairly distinct zones of high, medium, and low levels of rainfall. Generally, land nearer to oceans receives more moisture, more evenly spread throughout the year. Land toward the center of continents receives less moisture and then only at certain times during the year.

There are plenty of exceptions to this. For instance, local rainfall patterns can be changed by mountains that force clouds to rise and release their moisture on one side, creating a dry rain shadow on the other. And south-facing slopes get more sun, which evaporates water, so they are warmer and drier than north-facing slopes. Forests grow in all but the coldest and driest environments.

Soil also plays a major role in determining where trees can grow. Soil is a product of the parent rock under it, the local climate, and the vegetation growing on it. Most plants are quite specific about how much moisture and nutrients they need, and different kinds of soil vary greatly in these resources. Grains of sand have large spaces between them, so sandy soil gives up water to plants easily. But it also loses the water quickly. A soil with lots of clay has tiny pores, holds water for a long time, but hangs on to it tenaciously. The situation with nutrients is similar. Some soils hold ample nutrients but release them very slowly. Others never hold many nutrients at any one time because they are constantly recycling them to plants.

Interactions between organisms can also affect the distribution of

South-facing slopes are often dry and warm. On this hillside trees grow only on the cool, moist, north-facing slope.

tree species. For example, deer graze on tree seedlings. In some areas, deer may destroy nearly all the young trees. But small animals, such as squirrels and birds, may carry the seeds of trees beyond where they would normally fall, thus spreading the tree species to new locations. Plants themselves compete for resources and may exclude each other from some areas.

Disturbances such as fire, windstorms, insects, and floods can

Old-growth Douglas-fir logs have accounted for about one-quarter of softwood production in the United States during the 20th century.

affect forest distribution as well. For example, regular fires are partly responsible for the border between prairie and deciduous forest in the midwestern United States. They kill tree seedlings, which are replaced by quick-sprouting grasses. Fire plays an important role in many forests, as we will see.

Humans interact with and disturb forests. Sometimes the interaction is mutually beneficial—when we manage forests wisely, replant areas that have been logged, or just leave a forest alone. Other times we are more of a catastrophic disturbance, destroying vast tracts of forest and causing the extinction of scores of plant and animal species.

Humans have changed forests throughout history. The ancient Greeks and other Mediterranean cultures faced severe timber shortages after cutting down large areas of forest. And Hadrian, the Roman emperor from A.D. 117 to 138, actually ordered the forested mountains of northern Lebanon set aside to yield a steady supply of timber for his warships. When England was invaded by the Romans two thousand years ago, it was a vast forest of mighty oak, beech, and basswood. By the Middle Ages, so much land had been cleared that there was less forest than there is today. In North America, Indians burned and cleared land for thousands of years. But their impact was small compared to that of other cultures around the world, and miniscule compared to the changes wrought by Europeans who arrived only a few centuries ago.

Humans continue to use and change forests. To use the earth's forest resources wisely, we must know where and how forests grow. Many geographers and botanists have set out to explore, map, and study the world's forests. Today we know where the major forest biomes occur, but we still have a lot to learn about how these forests work.

In the following chapters we will explore four important forest biomes: boreal, temperate coniferous, coniferous rain forest, and deciduous.

1 / The Boreal Forest

Boreal forests are found in cold northern climates. Low temperatures in winter are often below -15° C (5° F), and summer temperatures rarely rise above 30° C (86° F). The growing season (the number of days between spring and fall frosts) ranges from 90 to 120 days. Only 15 to 20 inches (40 to 50 cm) of moisture fall each year. But the forest appears wet because little water evaporates at such low temperatures, and for much of the year it is frozen.

The trees of the boreal forest are mostly conifers. Pine trees are conifers. So are spruce and fir, which are often used for Christmas trees. These trees produce their seeds from cones instead of flowers. In contrast to deciduous trees, which drop their leaves each fall, most coniferous trees keep their needle-like leaves all year by constantly replacing needles that fall.

A Vast Wilderness

The boreal forest biome is the northern extension of the temperate evergreen forest. It covers 4.6 million square miles (12 million square kilometers), or about one-quarter of all the forested land in the world. This type of forest stretches all the way around the northern part of the world, from Canada and Alaska to the U.S.S.R. and Scandinavia.

To the north of the boreal forest biome lies the tundra. Along the

17

broad border, or ecotone, of these two great biomes the trees become smaller and smaller and the forest is sometimes called taiga. The trees begin to resemble shrubs and finally give way to arctic tundra. Toward the south, the boreal forest blends subtly into the forests of the Pacific Northwest, Northeast United States and the grasslands of the mid-continent. Conifers similar to those of the boreal forest also grow in the higher elevations of many mountain ranges far to the south of the actual boreal forest biome.

Because of the short growing season, low levels of light, and cold temperatures, boreal trees are small compared to conifers further south. They rarely reach above 60 feet (about 20 meters) or grow more than 2 feet (60 centimeters) in diameter. But they make the most of the few warm days they get. Because evergreen conifers keep their needles all year, they can begin photosynthesis and growth during the

A spruce forest on the edge of a bog.

first warm days of spring. Deciduous trees, on the other hand, must wait for new leaves to emerge and grow.

Walking through a boreal forest might seem boring since there are few tree species, often just spruce and fir. And in many places the forest goes on monotonously, mile after mile, with little change in the small size or slender pointed shape of the trees. The understory also has few species, mostly low evergreen shrubs and herbs, and thick carpets of moss on the ground.

These forests may seem simple, but they are also wild. Few people

Only mosses and a few small shrubs grow under the canopy of this boreal forest.

Moose prefer wet areas and often graze on aquatic vegetation.

live this far north. The virgin forest is vast, and animals roam freely. Caribou and musk-ox thrive on a diet of mosses and lichens, many of which grow on the trees themselves. Grizzly and black bears are common. Snowshoe hares, the most abundant primary consumer, are the favorite food of the lynx, a northern cousin of the bobcat. Arctic and red foxes feed more on smaller prey while wolves are quite versatile; they eat whatever they can get, from young or weak caribou and deer to field mice.

Pound for pound, the most ferocious predator in the boreal forest is the wolverine, the largest member of the weasel family, weighing in at 24 to 40 pounds (11 to 18 kilograms). They have been known to attack full-grown moose which stand six feet (two meters) tall at the shoulder. Usually they are less ambitious, but even so they often chase a grizzly bear or a wolf away from its kill. Closer to water live beaver, muskrat, otter, and mink. Moose also frequent wetter habitats.

Water and Fire

The boreal forest biome in the central and western parts of North America gets little rainfall compared to that on the East Coast. But the ground is often wet or soggy anyway because water is frozen for much of the year and evaporates slowly in the cool climate. Also, the trees use little water, both because they grow slowly and because they cannot take up frozen water.

Soils are usually infertile for several reasons. Excess water leaches nutrients away from roots. More importantly, the wet cold environment slows down the activity of decomposers (the small animals, bacteria and fungi in the soil that digest, break down and recycle dead animals and plants). So nutrient-rich dead matter piles up on the forest floor and recycles slowly.

Most of the needles, branches, and tree trunks that accumulate on the ground are flammable, especially during a dry spell. The result is that widespread forest fires are started by lightning storms. The fires can burn thousands of acres before they are even spotted, and most forest stands burn every fifty to two hundred years. Individual fires commonly burn 10,000 acres (4,000 hectares), and severe ones may burn 100 to 200 square miles (250 to 500 square kilometers).

But the trees in these forests are adapted to fire. Some of the pines, which grow on drier sandy soil, need fire to burn the sticky resins off their cones. This allows the cones to open and release their seeds. Although fire usually kills spruce and fir trees, their seeds often survive to start a new forest. Before these young conifers mature, short-lived deciduous trees take over for a few decades. The most important of these deciduous trees are aspen, with its fluttering heart-shaped leaves, and paper birch, so named because of its white papery bark, which was used by Native Americans to make canoes.

These fast-growing deciduous trees retain nutrients released by fires and prevent soil from washing away. Eventually they are over-topped by the slower-growing conifers, and most die from old age and

This aerial photo shows a recently burned area in the center of a boreal forest. A small wetland is at the bottom of the photo.

lack of light. But there are usually a few survivors to provide seeds when a fire opens up some space. They are also prolific sprouters; if the trunk of the tree is destroyed but the roots survive, aspens grow new stems from the roots and birches grow them from the stump.

The cold wet weather, lack of nutrients, and frequent fire limit the growth of these forests. An average hectare (equal to 2.5 acres or about 2 football fields) of boreal forest supports about 200 metric tons (440,000 pounds) of biomass, and grows an additional 8 metric tons each year. It would take fifteen hundred people crowded onto a football field to achieve a biomass of 200 metric tons per hectare. Even so, this is less than half of the biomass and yearly growth of a typical tropical forest.

Forest Products

Much of the world's timber comes from boreal forests, especially from the southern half where the trees are bigger. This is because conifer woods such as spruce, fir, and pine make good building material. They also are easy to work with; hence they are known as softwoods. (In contrast, many deciduous trees such as maple, oak, and ash have harder, denser wood and are known as hardwoods.) The wood of many boreal species can be polished to a beautiful blond color, so it makes attractive furniture.

Boreal conifers such as spruce and fir also yield superior wood pulp for making paper. The paper of this book is made from wood pulp. To make this paper, a tree is cut down, chipped into small pieces, and then boiled to a pulp in chemicals. The chemicals remove substances such as lignin, but leave the main ingredient—cellulose. The wood pulp is then poured over a wire screen on which the cellulose fibers are trapped while most of the liquid passes through. The wet mat of fibers is pressed between felt rollers to squeeze more liquid out and then dried. Finally it is spun on to huge rolls of paper 8 to 24 feet wide.

Most people know that paper is made from trees, but not many are aware that the idea was unheard of only one hundred and fifty years ago. Back then paper was made of rags, seed hairs of cotton, straw, and old paper. In the mid-1800s, rags were often in short supply and the pulp of trees was used as a substitute and out of desperation. The chemical process was invented in Germany, but it was first put to use on a large scale in the frontier towns of western North America where newspaper publishers needed paper.

Paper made from tree pulp is good enough for newsprint, but most high-quality paper is made from a mixture of wood pulp, rags, and other sources of fiber. The source of pulp, the chemicals used to treat the pulp, and the bleaching process determine the quality of the paper. Paper products include writing paper, newspaper, cardboard, tissue paper, coffee filters, lampshades, and even clothing. The average person in the United States uses over 500 pounds (230 kilograms) of paper each year.

But paper is only one of many products made from cellulose. Wood pulp can be treated with more chemicals to yield long fibers, pellets, and wide sheets of cellulose acetate, a plastic. The fibers are used to make cigarette filters and can be woven into rayon cloth. The pellets are molded into tooth brushes, combs, tool handles, lampshades, buttons, and many more everyday items. The clear sheets may be dyed and used as light filters or transparencies for overhead projectors. Video and audio tapes are made from very thin sheets that have been chemically altered to cellulose nitrate. This same substance also makes up about 60 percent of the explosive charge in bullet cartridges.

Boreal forests account for over a quarter of all forested land in the world. The vast Siberian boreal forest in the U.S.S.R. is larger than the entire United States. Huge areas remain wild, but as forests elsewhere are depleted, these boreal ecosystems may be called upon to supply even more wood products. Some of these forests' wild character will doubtless be lost. With careful management, however, many of these forests can provide both timber and habitat for wild creatures.

2/Temperate Coniferous Forests

Temperate coniferous forests cover about 3.5 million square miles (more then 5 million square kilometers) of the earth's surface. This amounts to 3.5 percent of the earth's land area and 10 percent of all the world's forests. They grow in most mountainous areas north of the equator, from the Himalayas to the Alps. Temperate coniferous forests even grow on the island of Crete in the Mediterranean and in Morocco's Atlas Mountains in North Africa.

In North America they are found from coastal British Columbia eastward to the Rocky Mountains, and southward to southern California and well into Mexico. Conifers are also important in the southeastern United States, where they are among the first trees to come back after a forest fire. On average, these forests contain 350 metric tons of living and dead biomass per hectare and produce an additional 13 metric tons per hectare each year. But these averages merely mask the incredible variety of temperate coniferous forests.

High, Dry Forests

Mountains and coniferous trees seem to go together. Many conifers can withstand a dry climate with warm or hot summers and cold snowy winters. This is mountain weather, and the coniferous forests growing here are known as montane forests at middle elevations and subalpine forests further up. Different species of juniper, pine, fir, and spruce can be found in certain elevation zones where the climate best suits them. Their small needle-leaves hold moisture much better than the paper-thin leaves of deciduous trees. A thick waxy cuticle provides extra protection from water loss.

Western North America contains more species of coniferous trees than any other place of the same size in the world. One reason may be that in the distant past, many conifers found refuge here when the

This montane coniferous forest of ponderosa pine in Arizona lets plenty of light into the understory.

climate elsewhere was not suitable for them. Another reason is that the rugged terrain and variable climate offer many different habitats for the different species.

The forests of San Francisco peaks in northern Arizona are a good example of how mountainous terrain results in many elevational zones of forest. At the base of the mountains, at about 5,000 feet (1,500 meters), the desert-like climate supports a sparse piñon-juniper woodland. Further up the mountainside, the woodland gives way to ponderosa pine in the cool ravines and north-facing slopes. From 7,000 to 8,000 feet (2,100 to 2,400 meters), ponderosa pine is the dominant tree, growing in stately open forests. As the climate gets cooler and moister at about 8,000 feet (2,400 meters), Douglas fir replaces the pines, first on the north-facing slopes and then everywhere.

Spruce and fir, the most common trees in the boreal forest, are found here and there at 9,000 feet (2,700 meters). From 9,500 feet (2,900 meters) on up they are the dominant trees in the subalpine forest. These spruce and fir trees are not the same species as their cousins to the north. Nevertheless these colder, wetter forests are essentially high elevation islands of boreal forest surrounded by montane forest. Limber pine and bristlecone pine grow in the rockier exposed places. Above 11,000 feet (3,350 meters) it is too windy and cold for trees to grow. But a few trees hang on up to 11,500 feet (3,500 meters) on the warmer south-facing slopes. Above the tree line is the alpine tundra.

Since it gets colder when we travel northward we might expect spruce and fir to be found at lower elevations in southern Alberta. Indeed, the spruce-fir forest here grows at 6,000 feet (1,800 meters) instead of 10,000 as in Arizona. On the other hand, if we were to travel south into the mountains of Mexico, we would find ponderosa pine growing at 10,000 feet (3,000 meters) instead of 7,500.

Animals of the montane coniferous forest are often adapted to a particular forest zone. For example, the noisy piñon jay lives in the warmer woodland at a lower altitude. The closely related Clark's nutcracker prefers the treeline. Also known as the "camp robber," this bird spends a lot of time in the fall stashing seeds which it will have a hard time finding under the winter snow. Larger animals such as deer and elk wander throughout these zones. Often they head for the high country in the summer and spend the coldest months at lower elevations in the pines, or even lower down.

Two tree species that have done particularly well around humans are lodgepole pine and aspen. As people settled the western mountains of North America, many fires were started by accident in mining and

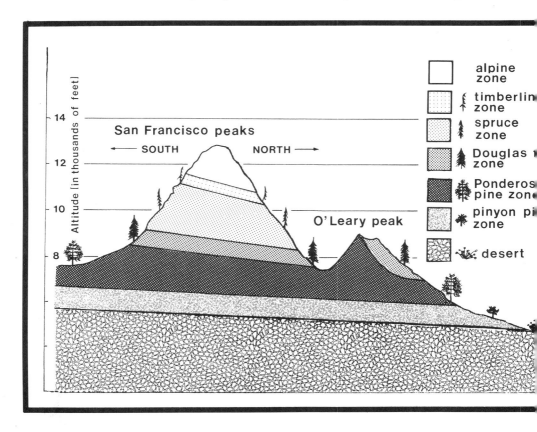

San Francisco peaks vegetation zones. The forest zones climb a little higher on the warmer south-facing slopes.

lumber camps. The cones of lodgepole pine require heat to open them, so these accidental fires gave this pine tree the chance it needed to replace spruce and fir in some areas.

Fire continues to play an important role in many coniferous forests. Nearly 1 million acres (400,000 hectares) or about 40 percent of Yellowstone National Park burned in 1988. Some people were understandably upset because of the loss of personal property and the apparent destruction of the forest. Yet fire is a natural event in most coniferous forests. A young, vigorous forest usually returns after fire.

The fluttering leaves of aspen trees were not nearly so common in montane forests a hundred years ago as they are now. Human-caused fire probably gave this fast-growing species a chance to spread by seed and by a very special method—clonal roots. As aspen roots spread away from the tree, new shoots sprout from the roots. These new shoots become trees with roots of their own, which in turn produce more shoots. In time, a single tree can give rise to a whole stand of trees, all genetically identical. This explains why one can see an entire hillside of aspen trees turn the same color of gold during the fall, while another turns orange and another crimson. Each patch of aspen, standing out from the dark green conifers, is really one genetic individual.

Southern Conifer Forests

Pine trees grow not only in the northern and western parts of North America, but in the southeastern states as well. The southeastern pines are quite different from those in the west and north. They thrive in a warm, moist climate, with plenty of light. Like many other conifers, they are colonizers, often invading after fire. After one-to-two hundred years, deciduous hardwood trees such as hickory, oak, and magnolia often overtop and shade out the pines. But if the fast-growing pines are replaced by more shade-loving hardwoods, why are there any pines at all in the southeast? There are several reasons.

Pines occur naturally in the Southeast because fires are common in that part of the country. Fire kills many of the deciduous trees and opens up places for the pines to grow. Many of these pines have ways of surviving fire. Long-leaf pine, for example, spends the first few years of its life growing a long tap root deep into the soil. Above the ground it hardly grows at all and looks more like a tuft of grass than a tree. Most fires just scorch the grassy tuft of needles without killing the root. Once the root is deep and strong and can gather plenty of nutrients, the tree shoots up rapidly. With luck, the tree will grow tall enough so that the branches will be above the next fire.

These slash pine trees in a southern coniferous forest in Georgia are used for making poles and turpentine.

Another reason pines are so common in the Southeast is that they grow as fast or faster than deciduous hardwoods on poor soil, especially on the coastal plain. In addition, much of this area was once farmed and, as soils deteriorated from overuse, farmers abandoned their land. Many farms were also ravaged during the Civil War. Pines, tolerating the poor soil better than most hardwoods, invaded this abandoned land.

Eventually the pines on the abandoned fields grew large enough to be harvested. Instead of letting pines invade again in a haphazard way, foresters planted the fastest-growing species. Because these southern pines grow so fast, they can be harvested in only twenty to forty years. Fast-growing trees have weaker, less dense wood than slow-growing ones, so a lot of the timber cut in the southeastern United States is used for making paper and other wood fiber products rather than lumber. However, new technology is producing improved fiberboard and plywood. These products rival the strength of solid wood, but can be made from smaller, fast-growing trees.

Thus a combination of fire, less fertile soil, farm abandonment, and plantings by foresters is responsible for the dominance of pine in many parts of the southeastern United States today. Of course pines grew in the Southeast before Europeans arrived. Back then Native Americans needed clear land to grow crops, so they set fires. Whenever these cleared lands were abandoned, pines were among the first trees to invade.

Although there were not as many pines in early colonial days as there are now, there were enough to attract Europeans for several reasons. One of the reasons the Europeans set out to the New World was to discover new sources of naval stores. This sticky resin was used to seal boats watertight, and pines provided the only source of such resins. Extracting it from pine trees soon became a major occupation for the colonists. It was also a messy one. Trees were felled, hauled to a large pit, and then burned. After that, workers would climb in and scrape the burned tar-like residue off the sides of the pit. North Carolinans are still nicknamed "Tarheels."

The Pine Barrens

Many pine forests in the southeastern United States are good examples of a landscape altered by humans. If you look closely, you will notice that the trees sometimes grow close together in rows. Foresters plant trees like this so that the trees will grow upward rapidly and be easy to harvest.

Plantations are less common on the poorest sandy soils. In these areas grow natural stands of pine. They grow better than most hardwoods on such soils, but not well enough to be worth much to a timber company or a forester.

One of the largest and most pristine coastal pine forests is the Pine Barrens in southern-central New Jersey. The soils here are sandy and acidic and range from very wet in low, swampy areas to porous and dry. Because the land is not fertile enough for agriculture or forestry, the stunted pine trees growing here have remained undisturbed by people. Thus we have an unusual wild area wedged between the urban areas of New York City and Philadelphia.

As these urban areas continue to grow, the Pine Barrens will come under more pressure. Most people recognize the fragile nature of the Pine Barrens, and for now this forest remains wild, yet easily accessible to millions of city dwellers.

3/Coniferous Rain Forests

Coniferous rain forests are often included in the temperate coniferous forest biome, but they are unique in many respects. The ample rain and mild climate allow the trees to grow to immense sizes and to live much longer than trees in most other forest biomes. In many of these forests the climate is mild enough for coniferous trees to grow nearly year round. Deciduous trees, which shed their leaves each fall, cannot take advantage of this long growing season. They also suffer more during periodic short, dry spells. So evergreen conifers usually dominate.

Coniferous rain forests are found in northwestern North America and in parts of Japan, New Zealand, and Tasmania. In North America these forests grow from southeastern Alaska to northern California. They include the coastal rain forests of Sitka spruce and western hemlock, the redwood fog-belt forests, and the hemlock-Douglas fir forests of the Coast and Cascade ranges.

Coastal Forests

From southeast Alaska along the coast of British Columbia, Washington, and Oregon the 60 to 160 inches (150 to 400 cm) of year-round rain supports a narrow band of Sitka spruce. This tree shares some space with hemlocks and cedars, but towers over both neighbors, reaching heights of up to 250 feet (75 meters). It grows quickly, but it does not do well under the shade of other trees.

Conifers are not the only trees in this rain-soaked realm. On recently disturbed sites, red alder, a deciduous tree, takes over and plays a key role in its short seventy-year life span. Alders do something that few other trees can: in their roots they harbor bacteria that capture nitrogen in large quantities and store it. When alders die and young conifers take over, this essential nutrient is released and helps the growing conifers to reach their tremendous heights.

Temperate coniferous rain forest in the Pacific Northwest. The Sitka spruce trees are growing in a line on an old log.

Big leaf maple is another deciduous tree that grows beneath the giant evergreens. It grows mainly in very moist ravines. Like spruce and hemlock, an alder or maple may support up to 100 pounds (45 kilograms) of mosses and other epiphytes. But these little broadleaved trees have adapted to their guests. They can send out roots from their branches and gather up nutrients that accumulate in the mosses.

Just a few miles inland, the rainfall decreases a little, allowing western hemlock to become dominant. Douglas fir edges into this habitat as well. An odd feature of these coastal forests is the way trees sometimes grow in neat rows. The explanation for this is surprisingly simple: periodic coastal windstorms knock over the tall spruces and hemlocks. But the dead giants continue to generate life because their moss-covered logs serve as nurseries to thousands of tiny hemlock and spruce seedlings. Long after the logs have rotted into the ground, a few seedlings will have survived to become towering giants growing in a line for up to 130 feet (40 meters) along the forest floor.

Fire and Old-Growth Forests

After crossing the Coast Range, the rainfall tapers off a little more. With less rainfall comes a greater chance of fire. Fire opens up the forest, letting in light, and it often burns through the debris on the forest floor to bare soil. These are perfect conditions for Douglas fir, whereas hemlock grows better in moist shade.

Immediately after fire, the ground is covered with herbs such as purple fireweed and yellow woodland groundsel. Hidden under this thick carpet are a few sprouts of plants whose roots survived the fire, and even some tree seedlings. But before these residual species can grow above the herbs, invaders such as bracken fern, thimbleberry and *Ceanothus* take over.

As these plants die back, alder may emerge for a few years and enrich the soil. Finally, three or four decades later, Douglas fir overtops an understory now composed mostly of residual shrubs. As the forest floor becomes more shaded and cool, and holds more moisture, hemlock begins to push up through the canopy. Given enough time and an absence of fire or windstorms, hemlock will dominate the stand. This sequence, from herbs to shrubs to alder through Douglas fir and ending with hemlock is an example of forest succession.

But because of fire this successional sequence rarely reaches its theoretical final stage or climax of hemlock. Most ecologists agree that the concept of a forest climax is more theoretical than real, mainly because fire and windstorms and diseases interrupt successional sequences so often.

Thus Douglas fir is the dominant tree in these forests even though hemlock, with its delicate foliage and droopy top, lives longer, often over a thousand years. Most Douglas fir-western hemlock forests never live a thousand years. Instead, a typical stand of trees might grow for two hundred fifty to six hundred years before a windstorm or fire starts the process of succession over again. Forests more than two hundred fifty years old are known as old-growth. They are very different from younger forests. The trees average about 3 to 6 feet (1 to 2 meters) in diameter and 200 to 250 feet (60 to 75 meters) in height.

Some trees are larger. The biggest ones were cut years ago when loggers took the best trees from the fertile lowland valleys. One logging crew in 1895 claimed to have cut down a 417-foot (127-meter) tall Douglas fir in British Columbia. The tree was 25 feet (7.6 meters) in diameter at the base.

A typical hectare (2.5 acres) of old-growth forest of four hundred years of age might support about 1,200 tons of biomass. The same forest at a hundred years would have about 600 tons of biomass. In contrast, a typical hectare of deciduous forest in eastern North America might have 160 tons, and the maximum would be about 400 tons.

The differences between old-growth and younger forests go beyond mere comparisons in size. Old-growth forests function differently. Instead of consisting of a uniform stand of young, rapidly growing trees, the forest becomes more complex. Deep shade here. A fallen log and a patch of sunlight there. As a forest approaches maturity, some trees die. A dead tree, or snag, may remain standing for almost a hundred years, providing food and shelter for various animals, from insects to woodpeckers. Eventually the snag falls to the ground where a whole new group of species takes over: microbes and insects slowly devour the wood, while small rodents, amphibians, even bear, bobcat, and skunk find food and shelter around the log.

The nutrients from giant logs slowly recycle back into the forest floor for hundreds of years as the rootlets of fir and hemlock invade the rotting wood. The log also acts like a giant sponge, soaking up water most of the year and slowly releasing it to the forest during dry spells.

The first branches of a large tree are often 100 feet (30 meters) above the forest floor. The massive canopy continues for another 100 feet. The sixty million needles of a single old Douglas fir take ad-

Old-growth Douglas fir-western hemlock forests are among the most magnificent and valuable on earth.

vantage of the mild climate to capture the sun's energy nearly year-round, instead of three to four months, as in many other temperate forests. The sunlight is often filtered through clouds and the canopy itself, so an old-growth forest puts out a vast collection system: the needles of a stand of trees may cover up to fifteen times as much area as the ground below. This is almost triple the leaf surface area of the typical deciduous forest.

Animal Life in Old-Growth Forests

High in the canopy live animals that have adapted remarkably to a world very different from that on the forest floor. The red tree vole depends mostly on needles for food, shelter, and water. The northern flying squirrel prefers seeds, but when these are not available during

The northern spotted owl hunts for small mammals found mostly in old-growth coniferous forests in the Pacific Northwest.

the winter, the squirrels get by on lichens growing in the canopy. These same lichens provide up to 3.5 pounds of nitrogen per acre (4 kilograms per hectare) to the forest. Pileated woodpeckers, nuthatches, and several species of warblers prefer large old trees for nesting and foraging. Some birds, such as Vaux's swift and the northern spotted owl, require old-growth forests for survival.

The secretive spotted owl is currently the center of much controversy. Because it is rare, most people agree that it should be protected. The only way to protect the birds is to preserve the forests where they live, but preserving these forests means not cutting the valuable trees.

Many people would like to log this timber. Others argue that 95 percent of the old-growth forests in the Pacific Northwest have already been cut, and that the remaining 5 percent should be saved for future generations to enjoy. To complicate things even more, both sides have made studies of how much territory the owl needs. Those who would save the owl believe each pair may need up to 2,200 acres (890 hectares) of forest. Those who favor logging believe a pair of owls needs only about 300 acres (120 hectares). To argue over which side is right misses the point.

The spotted owl is but one animal in a complex and poorly understood web of life that runs throughout the forest. The important question is, "How important are our old-growth forests to us?" How much do we value them for their biological attributes versus the value of the timber they contain? Can we even put a price on the deep silent beauty of an old-growth forest, or on the plants, birds, mammals, insects, fungi, and microorganisms that live there?

For now the U.S. Forest Service, which owns most of the remaining old-growth has decided to cut less timber in order to protect the spotted owl. This will likely cost many loggers their jobs, but with few old-growth forests left, the days of logging these giant trees are numbered anyway. The timber industry is beginning to harvest old-

Old-growth redwoods, the tallest living organisms on earth, are found in Northern California.

growth in ways that preserve habitat for plants and animals, and to convert to cutting smaller more plentiful trees.

Giant and Ancient Trees

South and east of the moist Pacific Northwest, the climate becomes drier and warmer. There are still pockets of cool, moist climate, such as the northern coast of California. These fog-shrouded hills and valleys are home to the world's tallest trees—the redwoods. These graceful giants may live more than two thousand years and reach heights of 330 feet (100 meters). The record is 368 feet, or about the size of a thirty-story building. And this tree is only six hundred years old. Redwoods grow quickly. On the best sites, they may reach 175 feet (50 meters) in height in only a hundred years. They thrive in the cool coastal fog but are adpated to periodic hot fires. If a fire kills a mature redwood, it does something few other conifers can. It usually sprouts, and a new generation encircles the old stump.

Even further south, and no longer in what we could consider a rain forest, grow the world's largest organisms. Giant sequoias do not grow as tall as redwoods, but they weigh more. The largest tree, the General Sherman is 32 feet (10 meters) in diameter and 272 feet (83 meters) tall. Individuals 275 feet tall, 20 feet in diameter, and weighing nearly 1 million pounds (220 metric tons) are common on the best sites. If one of these trees were cut and used for lumber, it would be enough to build fifty three-bedroom homes.

But this should never happen, because the few remaining groves of giant sequoias are protected within national parks. Without humans to end their lives prematurely, little else can keep these giants from living up to four thousand years. Not even fire is much of a threat. The 1- to 3-foot (30- to 90-cm)-thick bark shields them from all but the most devastating blazes. Giant sequoias are not the longest-lived trees, though. This record belongs to the small and gnarled bristlecone pine, which lives high up near timberline, where trees give way to alpine tundra. These trees may live as long as eight thousand years.

4/Temperate Deciduous Forests

Temperate deciduous forest covers the eastern half of the United States, extending from eastern Texas to the Great Lakes and into southeastern Canada. This biome is also found in Asia from southeastern Siberia to southern-central China and in Europe. The European temperate forests, however, contain fewer kinds of trees than those in North America and eastern Asia. Temperate deciduous forests cover about 4.3 million square miles (7 million square kilometers) of the earth's surface. They account for about 15 percent of all the world's forests. Most of these forests have been cut down to make way for farms, towns, and cities, but much still remains or has grown back.

Deciduous Trees

The term deciduous (from a Latin word meaning "to fall from") refers to the leaves that fall from the trees each autumn. Oaks, maples, beech, birches, ash, and hickories are some of the more familiar deciduous trees.

Deciduous trees grow well in a climate with warm summers, cool winters, and year-round moisture. But the climate of the eastern North American deciduous forests ranges from the warm humid summers and frigid winters of southeastern Canada to the hot summers and mild winters of the southern states. So it is not surprising that there are many types of deciduous forests in this area.

In a typical deciduous forest in the temperate zone, the tallest trees usually reach 60 to 100 feet (20 to 30 meters) above the ground. The largest trunks may be 3 feet (1 meter) or more in diameter, but most are smaller, ranging from 5 to 20 inches (10 to 50 centimeters). Scattered among these trees may be a few conifers such as hemlock or pine.

Smaller trees grow in the cool shade of the canopy; under them grow saplings, shrubs, and herbs. At each level, from the treetops to the ground, the environment changes. Under the canopy there is less light, temperatures are lower, the wind is gentler. Rain is caught by the tree tops and falls to the ground in large droplets or runs down the trunks of the trees. Light, the source of all energy in a forest, decreases steadily, going from full sunlight at the tops of the trees to only 1 to 5 percent of full sunlight at the forest floor.

The small shrubs and herbs on the forest floor usually get only flecks of sunlight that dapple their leaves for a few minutes or even seconds. They must respond rapidly to these bursts of light and capture what energy they can.

We rarely see life under the forest floor. It is hidden and the animals are small. Ecologists have found that roots alone account for 20 percent of all the living biomass in a forest, but most of a tree's roots spread only as far as it branches. About 90 percent of a tree's roots can be found in the top 8 inches (20 centimeters) of soil. Most of these roots are less than a few millimeters in diameter. Despite their small size, these fine roots have an enormous surface area so they can take up water and nutrients. The roots under 10 square feet (1 square meter) of the forest floor may have a surface area equal to the floor space of the average house.

Seasons
One thing that sets a deciduous forest apart from coniferous forests is

that we can more easily see distinct seasons. Most of us think of forests as green, shady places. In a deciduous forest this is true for about four to five months of the year. When the trees lose their leaves in the autumn, the forest environment feels more light and airy. Where one could have seen for only a few meters, now the view extends through the woods and over to the next ridge. The dry leaves and twigs crackling underfoot are somewhat flammable. The chance of a forest fire is highest in these forests at this time of year, yet fire is less common in deciduous forests than in coniferous forests.

While the leaves turn brilliant hues of crimson, orange, and yellow, the trees prepare for winter and the following spring. Deciduous trees avoid the cost of maintaining their leaves in the winter when sunlight is weak, temperatures low, and water scarce. Instead, the leaves drop off, the scars are sealed, and moisture is retained. Food

Deciduous forests in early spring are open with plenty of light (left), but just a few weeks later, all the trees and shrubs have grown new leaves, and the forest is much darker (right).

is stored in the branches and trunk, and next year's leaves and flowers are pre-formed and protected in thousands of buds.

Many trees shed their fruit at this time of year. The winged seeds of the maple spin to the ground like helicopters, while tiny birch seeds may blow hundreds of meters before landing. The acorns of various oak trees may be impossible to find, so highly prized are they by birds, squirrels, and other rodents.

These animals survive on seeds and fruits during the winter, whereas most reptiles and some mammals, such as the groundhog and jumping mouse, hibernate—that is, their metabolism slows down, their body temperature becomes lower, and they go into a deep sleep. They survive on fat stored in their bodies.

Many birds avoid the lean times of winter and fly south during the fall. Other birds—chickadees, nuthatches, wrens, and woodpeckers—stay around. They forage for buds on trees and shrubs, or hunt for insects hiding under the bark of trees. Most insects either lay eggs and die, burrow into the soil, or go into a pupal stage that can survive the cold temperatures.

Many mammals remain active. Foxes continue to hunt small rodents and deer forage on winter buds and evergreen shrubs; during the summer, they also eat grasses. White-tailed deer can be found throughout the deciduous forest. Their antlers are the most rapidly growing bone among mammals, taking only four months to reach full size: they shed them each year from December to February and then grow a new rack. Many people believe they can determine the age of a buck (male deer) by the number of points on his antlers. This is only partly true; the growth of antlers is influenced as much by diet and heredity as by age. Wildlife biologists tell the age of deer by their teeth, not by their antlers. Bucks use their antlers only once during the year, during the fall rutting (mating) season. The 200 pound (90 kilogram) males square off to compete for smaller 100 pound (45 kilogram) females. Sometimes the males' antlers become permanently locked, and both combatants slowly starve to death.

Deer are most active at night, just after sundown and just before sunrise, and often bed down at dawn. They prefer farmlands and open woods most of the year, but herd together under the protective forest canopy in the winter. Humans have provided deer with plenty of open brushy land in the last two hundred years.

We have also helped their populations to grow by getting rid of wolves, mountain lions, and coyotes. More deer live in eastern North America today than when European colonists first arrived. In the northeastern United States alone, hunters kill about 150,000 to 300,000 deer annually, but this is just a fraction of the population, which numbers in the low millions. In some areas their appetite for young sapling trees has prevented forests from growing naturally. In these areas deer are considered pests, and many biologists would like to decrease their numbers.

Some people object to reducing deer herds because they want plenty of deer to hunt. And some animal rights groups also object to reducing the herds because they do not want any deer killed. So for the forseeable future, deer populations will remain high.

As spring approaches, rainfall increases in some places. Coupled with melting snow in northern areas, the excess water can wash away soil and nutrients. Since most trees have yet to grow leaves in early spring, they cannot transpire through their leaves and take up the extra water from the soil. However, early flowering herbs and shrubs take advantage of the ample light that penetrates the leafless canopy. They quickly grow leaves and blossom. This short burst of activity requires some water. But most of the water from rain and melting snow runs into streams and rivers, swelling them to their limit.

The Dynamic Forest

This cycle of growth, storage, dormancy, and renewal repeats itself year after year. Eventually the larger trees mature, grow old, and die. Unless a wildfire or windstorm sweeps through the forest, the large old trees do not all die at once. Instead they weaken, die, and fall to

White-tailed deer are common throughout the deciduous forest.

the forest floor one by one, here and there, over decades or centuries. Each fallen tree leaves a gap in the canopy which allows more light to reach the forest floor.

At first grasses, herbs, and light-loving shrubs grow quickly and fill the space left by the fallen tree. If there is enough light, pioneer trees such as paper birch, with its light mobile seed, or pin cherry begin to push through the shrubs. These trees may dominate for a few decades. But they have short life spans and their own seedlings cannot live in their shade, so other trees more tolerant of shade join them. Finally, the old gap is likely to be filled by one or two of the most shade-tolerant trees.

In a few square miles of forest we would see different stages of this scenario occurring simultaneously. In one place a patch of forest contains very large old trees. Just a few meters away young trees push up through the branches of an old giant that has recently fallen. At another spot a large tree is about to die. Somewhere else, shade-tolerant trees are overtopping the pioneer trees. The result is a shifting mosaic of different sizes, ages, and species of trees. Overall the forest remains about the same: for each individual that dies, another similar individual is entering the canopy somewhere else. That is, the forest is in a steady state.

This steady state can be interrupted by fire, windstorms, attack by insects, sudden change in climate or through clearing by humans. Which trees survive or return depends on how severe, frequent, and widespread these disturbances are. For example, a light fire may remove just enough vegetation for pin-cherry seeds buried in the soil to take advantage of the increased light. A windstorm might knock down all trees taller than 50 feet (15 meters), but leave smaller ones undamaged. At the extreme, a very hot fire (a rare event in deciduous forests) might burn through the leaves, twigs, and other rotting matter on the forest floor to expose mineral soil. About the only seeds and seedlings that could grow here would be those of pine and birch.

But forests respond to even more far-reaching events than fire or windstorms. Trees also react to long-term climatic change. For example, most trees growing today in the Great Lakes region survived only in the southern United States during the height of the last Ice Age, about eighteen thousand years ago. As temperatures warmed, tree populations began to shift northward. By five thousand years ago, most tree species had spread through seed dispersal and other means to their present locations, some moving faster than others. Oaks reached the southern Great Lakes about nine thousand years ago, but chestnuts did not get there until two thousand years ago. Biologists still are not sure why.

Thus the eastern deciduous forest we see today is a product of many things—light, temperature, rainfall, moisture, and nutrients in the soil—which all change daily, monthly, and yearly. The fall of a

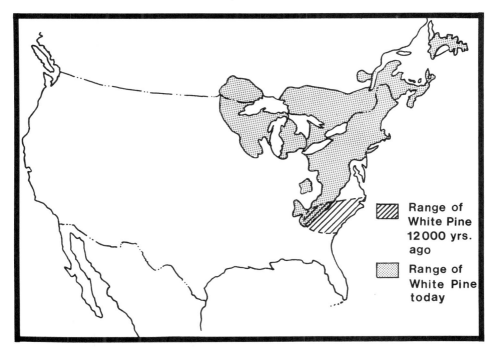

Many trees, like white pine, have moved northward since the last ice age ended 12,000 years ago.

single tree, or a storm, or a fire alters the amount of light, moisture, and nutrients available to trees and other plants. Animals gathering food for winter may carry seeds to new locations and help a species increase its range. And over the centuries the climate may change so much that tree species may migrate thousands of kilometers.

Today, the earth's climate may be changing faster than ever before. In the last century, pollutants from factories, automobiles, and even private homes have entered our environment.

Many of these chemicals remain in the atmosphere. These chemicals allow more of the sun's energy to penetrate our atmosphere, but they also retain heat rising from the ground. The result is a global temperature rise, known as the greenhouse effect. Small temperature variations of 2° or 3°C over thousands of years have caused tree species to migrate thousand of kilometers. Imagine what a larger increase in temperature within a few hundred years might do.

Some of the chemicals in the atmosphere are washed from the air in the form of acid rain. Many aquatic organisms, especially fish, have been killed by acid rain in the past decade. Scientists are less sure about the effect on trees. Acid rain by itself probably does not kill trees, but it may weaken them by damaging foliage and changing the chemical balance of the soil. When a severe storm, fire, or insect attack comes along, these weak trees are more likely to die.

5/One Biome, Many Forests

What would we find if we were to explore the eastern deciduous forest today? Starting from the same place on Manhattan Island as an early settler might have, we would have to search hard for natural forests. Still, in spite of the changes Europeans have wrought, much of eastern North America is still forested. If we were to travel northward we would find deciduous trees such as sugar maple, red maple, yellow birch, paper birch, and beech mingling with conifers such as pine, hemlock, spruce, and cedar. The combination of deciduous and coniferous trees in this region makes it a zone of transition between the boreal forest to the north and the lush deciduous forests to the south.

The Yankee Forest

Many trees in the northern third of the deciduous forest are famous for their brilliant fall colors: the orange and gold sugar maples, scarlet red maples, burnt-orange oaks, yellow birches, and rust-colored beeches. Surprisingly, the colors we see in the fall have been there all year long. They were merely hidden by the dominant green of the pigment chlorophyll. When the trees stop producing chlorophyll in the fall, the other colors begin to show through.

Early colonists in New England paid a price for these fall colors. The winters that followed were usually harsh, and the short summers

51

made growing anything but trees difficult. It took two men over a month to cut down just 2.5 acres (1 hectare) of forest, remove the stumps, and prepare the soil for planting. If the soil was especially rocky, as in New England, all the stones had to be removed. The stones were used to make walls to mark boundaries and to keep stray animals out of the crops.

Once the fertile Midwest was opened up in the mid-1800s, the rocky hill farms of New England could not compete. Many of the early colonial farms were abandoned. White pines and birches began to reclaim the land. Today we can walk through dense woods where once a colonist might have been able to see across miles of open fields in any direction. Many New England towns are crisscrossed with hundreds of miles of stone walls that are slowly and quietly crumbling in the forest.

These forests have not been completely abandoned. Landowners still harvest the trees, and some still run small farms. One activity has probably been going on in this area since Native Americans first arrived: the making of maple syrup and sugar from the sap of sugar maple trees.

Sugaring is done in the spring when the days reach 5° C (40° F) and the nights dip below freezing. The sweet sap can be intercepted on its way from the roots by drilling a shallow hole in the tree trunk, tapping in a spout, and letting the sap run into buckets. The 20 to 40 gallons (75 to 150 liters) of sap produced by one tree during the spring is enough to make 1/2 to 1 gallon (2 to 4 liters) of maple syrup.

If we were to travel across the Appalachians to the Midwest, we would find that trees such as maple, beech, and basswood grow much taller than in the north, mainly because of the fertile soil and warmer climate. As we approach the prairie, trees become smaller because of the drier climate. The dry climate also allows fire to burn more easily. This favors grasses over tree seedlings. Most of the trees along the ecotone between the forests and the prairie are oaks. They look more like shrubs than trees.

Oak Forests and the Chestnut Blight

If we headed south, we would find that temperatures are warmer still and rainfall more plentiful. Perhaps most important, the growing season is sometimes twice as long as in the north. The soils contain less organic matter and a thinner litter layer. This is because the warm, moist climate allows microorganisms to decompose dead leaves and twigs more rapidly into usable nutrients. These nutrients are rapidly cycled back into the vegetation.

Most of this southern deciduous forest can be classified as oak-hickory or oak-chestnut forest; however, the latter type of forest no longer exists. The American chestnut tree once was one of the

Every spring in the deciduous forest, sugar maples are tapped and their sap is boiled down to maple syrup.

dominant trees in the eastern deciduous forest. Chestnuts were common on slopes and ridges, especially in the central Appalachians. Here their creamy white blossoms could be seen towering over the other trees for miles away in early summer.

Chestnuts commonly grew taller than 80 feet (25 meters) and broader than 3 feet (1 meter) through the trunk. The largest trees reached over 100 feet (30 meters) in height, and had trunks over 10 feet (3 meters) in diameter. The huge logs were easily milled, and the light strong wood could be used for almost any purpose, from telegraph poles and railroad ties to fine furniture and musical instruments. Chestnut trees were also the primary source of tannin for tanning leather.

Chestnuts were an integral part of the forest community. Each fall they provided a reliable crop of nuts sought after by all animals: deer, woodpeckers, wild turkeys, raccoons, crows, foxes, and others. Bears fattened up for the winter on the nuts and often settled in for their winter's slumber in the hollow of a big chestnut tree. Roasted chestnuts and chestnut stuffing were traditions around most holiday tables. The nuts of this tree were smaller than those from Europe and China but they were far tastier.

Sadly it was one of these foreign chestnut trees that brought a deadly fungus with it to New York City in 1904. The blight spread rapidly and decimated the American chestnut population in just a few decades. Because the fungus can live only above ground, the roots of many chestnuts survived. But whenever they sprout a new shoot, the fungus quickly attacks. In many places these shortlived sprouts are the only remnants of this once dominant giant. This majestic tree may one day return, however. Scientists are working to cross-breed American chestnuts with the blight-resistant Chinese chestnut; and they are looking for new ways to control the fungus itself.

Today oaks are the most common trees in the central and southern part of the deciduous forest. But other species play important roles. Hickories have accompanied oaks in replacing the blighted chestnut.

Even without the American chestnut, deciduous forests are magnificent in the central Appalachians.

The richest of these forests are found in coves, or valleys, in the Great Smoky and Cumberland mountains. Here one commonly finds twenty-five to thirty species of trees in a single valley. No one species dominates the entire cove; instead, species grow where the environment best suits them. Oak-chestnut forests were once common on dry hillsides. Sweet buckeye favors fertile, well-drained sites. At higher

Massive chestnut trees were once dominant in much of the deciduous forest. An imported fungus wiped them out around 1915-1925.

elevations where temperatures are lower, northern species such as birch and sugar maple grow.

At the highest elevations grows Fraser fir, a close cousin to balsam fir, one of the dominant trees in the northern boreal forest. Indeed, the high-elevation forest of the central Appalachians is essentially an island of boreal forest surrounded by deciduous forest below.

These high-elevation forests are especially sensitive to acidic fog and mist, which often shrouds the mountain tops. In the past few decades many trees have died. Scientists are studying these and other forests to see if acid rain makes the trees more likely to die under the stressful conditions found at higher elevations.

Bottomland deciduous forests are common along river floodplains in the southeastern United States.

Bottomland Forests

If we continue south from the deciduous forest, we cross the broad band of pine forests described in Chapter 2. Interfingered into these pine forests, mainly along river floodplains, are bottomland forests.

The kinds of trees growing in these bottomland forests depend on subtle changes in the shape of the land. Low-lying land is flooded most of the year, so little oxygen reaches the trees' roots. Swamp forests of tupelo and bald cypress (a conifer) tolerate these conditions. In dense stands, few understory plants can survive, and tree seeds must wait for a dry spell to germinate. Slightly higher ground, where flooding occurs only part of the year, supports hardwood bottom forests of sweet gum, red maple, several kinds of oak, elm, and other species. A few feet higher grow ridge-bottom forests of sweet gum, oak, hickory, pecan, and even magnolia and beech. These forests are dry most of the year and support large trees up to 3 feet (1 meter) in diameter and 100 feet (30 meters) tall.

Further up-slope, in ravines and on river bluffs, broad-leaved evergreen magnolias mingle with deciduous beech and oak. And toward the coast we find evergreen live oaks, festooned with hanging Spanish moss. These forests represent a transition from the deciduous to the broad-leaved evergreen forest biome. Broad-leaved evergreen trees have broad, flat leaves like trees in the deciduous forest; but they keep their leaves year round. The leaves do fall from the trees, but they fall one by one rather than all at once, and they are continually replaced.

There are many types of broad-leaved evergreen forest, such as the live-oak forests of the Gulf Coast, the subtropical hammocks of South Florida, and the vast tropical forests of South America, Asia, and Africa. They all have one thing in common: a more constant climate than temperate forests. Instead of warm and cold seasons, these forests more often have a rainy season and a dry season.

57

6/Future Forests

Forests biomes north of the tropics are incredibly diverse: cool boreal forests, towering conifers, and deciduous forests that shed and grow new leaves every year. We have explored some major forest biomes, yet we've had to exclude others. The many types of mixed deciduous-coniferous forests of California are too numerous and varied to be included in this book. In addition, no attempt has been made to describe tropical forests; these complex ecosystems require an entire book of their own.

Yet these and other forests not mentioned in this book share many characteristics. They harness energy from the sun. They cycle nutrients. They regulate their environment. They provide people with food, shelter, and fuel. As long as there are forests, people will use them. Each year enough trees are cut throughout the world to build over 125 million single-family houses.

To use the earth's forest resources wisely, we must be aware of both the similarities and differences between forests. For example, many coniferous forests are adapted to occasional fire, whereas fire rarely occurs in some deciduous forests. Some forests can be harvested every forty years, whereas others must grow longer before they are ready for cutting. Still others, the most rare and fragile forests, are best left uncut.

We have seen how most temperate forests have been changed by humans. We still wonder what some of the original forests must have been like. What was it like to gather the fruit of 100-foot-(30-meter-) tall American chestnuts? What was the original forest of New England before the colonists arrived? Were some Douglas fir trees really taller than redwoods?

We have barely begun to explore some forest ecosystems. In a sense, biologists delving into the mysteries of these forests today are in a position similar to that of an early settler in North America, looking out over a pristine wilderness. They have a chance to know fragments of these biomes in their natural state.

There must be a balance between timber harvesting and forest preservation. The question is, "What agenda best ensures a steady supply of timber products, a healthy environment, and the protection of our remaining natural forests?"

Patch clearcuts in valuable old-growth Douglas-fir forests. How much should we cut and how fast? How much should be left alone?

Glossary

biomass—The weight of an organism, usually the total weight of all the living organisms in a community.

biome—A major regional community with its own type of climate, vegetation, and animal life.

community—A group of plants and animals interacting with one another in the same environment.

coniferous—Refers to trees whose reproductive parts are borne on cones, usually with evergreen needle-like leaves.

consumer—An organism that feeds on other living organisms.

deciduous—Refers to trees that shed their leaves before the winter or dry season.

decomposer—An organism that feeds on dead organic material, breaking it down into simpler substances and bringing about decay.

ecosystem—A community of organisms and their environment.

ecotone—A transitional zone separating two biomes.

evergreen—A woody plant that keeps its foliage throughout the year by continuously shedding and replacing a few leaves at a time.

forest—A major community in which the dominant plants are trees whose leafy crowns touch each other.

habitat—The area in which an organism or group of organisms live.

hardwoods—Usually refers to deciduous trees which grow more slowly and produce harder, denser wood than evergreen conifers.

montane forest—A forest growing in mountainous regions well below timberline.

old growth—Forests of large, old trees, usually more than two hundred and fifty years of age; old-growth forests are rare today.

softwoods—Evergreen coniferous trees that produce less dense, softer wood than most deciduous trees.

species—A group of populations genetically isolated from other such groups; for example, humans, chimpanzees, white-tailed deer, red oak, and white pine are all different species.

subalpine forest—A forest growing in mountainous regions near or just below timberline.

succession—A series of changes in the composition of plants and animals in an area beginning with colonization and ending with a stable climax.

taiga—Boreal forest, sometimes used to refer to the northern border of the boreal forest adjacent to the arctic tundra.

timberline—The line that marks the northerly, southerly, or altitudinal limit of tree cover.

tundra—A major biome where temperatures are so low that only lichens, mosses, heaths, sedges, grasses, and a few herbaceous plants can grow.

Further Reading

Black, David, and Anthony Huxley. *Plants*. New York: Facts on File, 1985.

Farb, Peter. *The Forest*. New York: Time, 1961.

List, Jr., Albert, and Ilka List. *A Walk in the Forest: The Woodlands of North America*. New York: Crowell, 1977.

McCormick, Jack. *The Life of the Forest*. New York. McGraw-Hill, 1966.

Newton, James R. *Forest Log*. New York: Crowell, 1980.

Pringle, Laurence. *Being a Plant*. New York: Crowell, 1983.

Pringle, Laurence. *Ecology, Science of Survival*. New York: Macmillan, 1971.

Pringle, Laurence. *Natural Fire: Its Ecology in Forests*. New York: Morrow, 1979.

Rushforth, Keith. *Trees*. New York: Exeter Books, 1983.

Scott, Jane. *Botany in the Field: An Introduction to Plant Communities for the Amateur Naturalist*. Englewood Cliffs, N.J.: Prentice-Hall, 1983.

Silverberg, Robert. *Vanishing Giants: The Story of the Sequoias*. New York: Simon & Shuster, 1969.

Zim, Herbert S., and Alexander C. Martin. *Trees: A Guide to Familiar American Trees*. New York: Golden Press, 1956.

Index